Skyscrapers

Magical

&

Glorious

PUBLISHER:SUPREME ART, USA

ISBN: 978-1942912798

About the Authors

Mohsen (Arash) Bahonar was born in Shiraz, Iran in 1980. Since he was a child he was interested in art and he did a lot of artwork such as inlay(khatam), mosaic, carving, painting, calligraphy, wooden girih tiler and design

He also started writing. Somayeh Mohammadi (Neda) was born in Esfahan, Iran in 1979. She was interested in art and. Poetry since she was a child. She studied architecture and did artwork and writing as well.

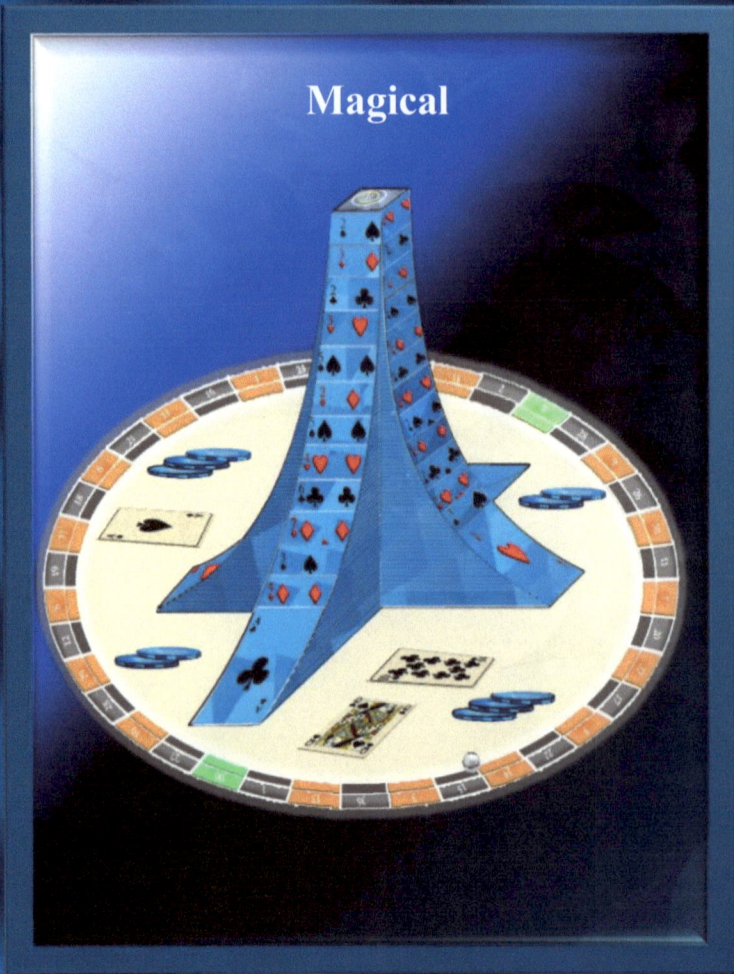

Magical

The idea of designing this building based on the play and happiness, which are two important human needs, came to my mind.

Play bring people together.

People of all ages need entertainment. Playing cards are one of the most popular gaming devices in the world. And I decided to design my building with playing cards.

Mohsen(Arash) Bahonar

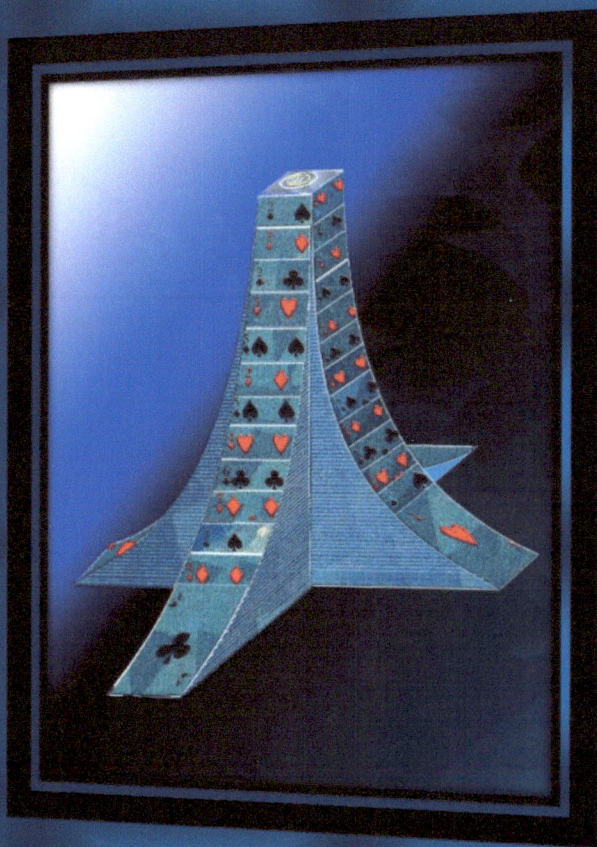

The building consist of four parts, and it can be built from thirty to three hundred floors.

The name of each part is inspired by the name of the game cards

(Heart, Spade, Diamond, Club)

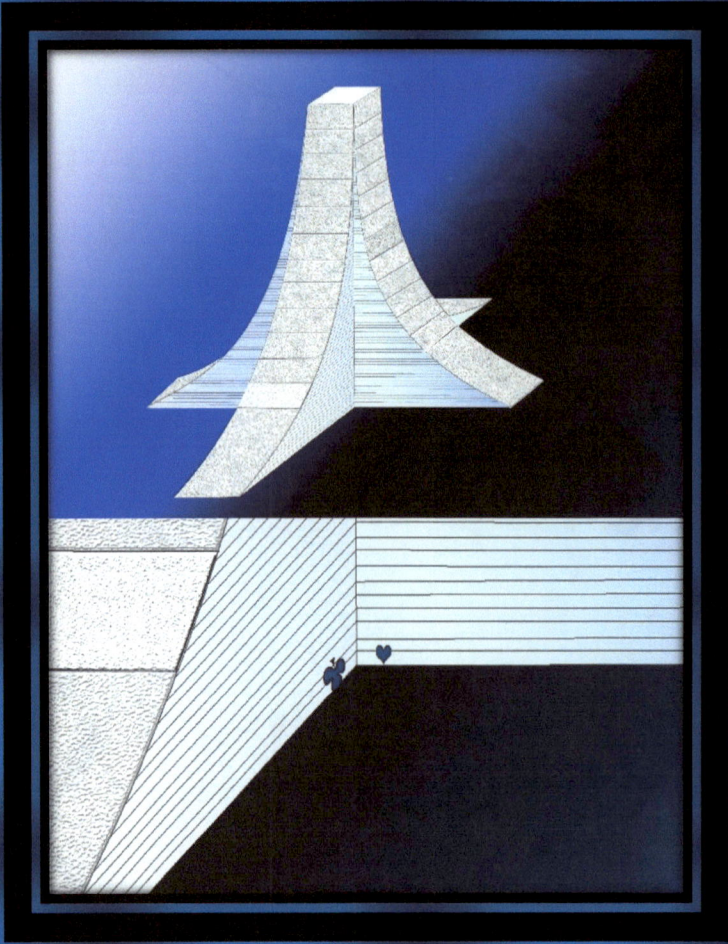

Each part of the building has two entrance and exit door.

The doors of each part of the building are designed in the shape of the name of the same part.

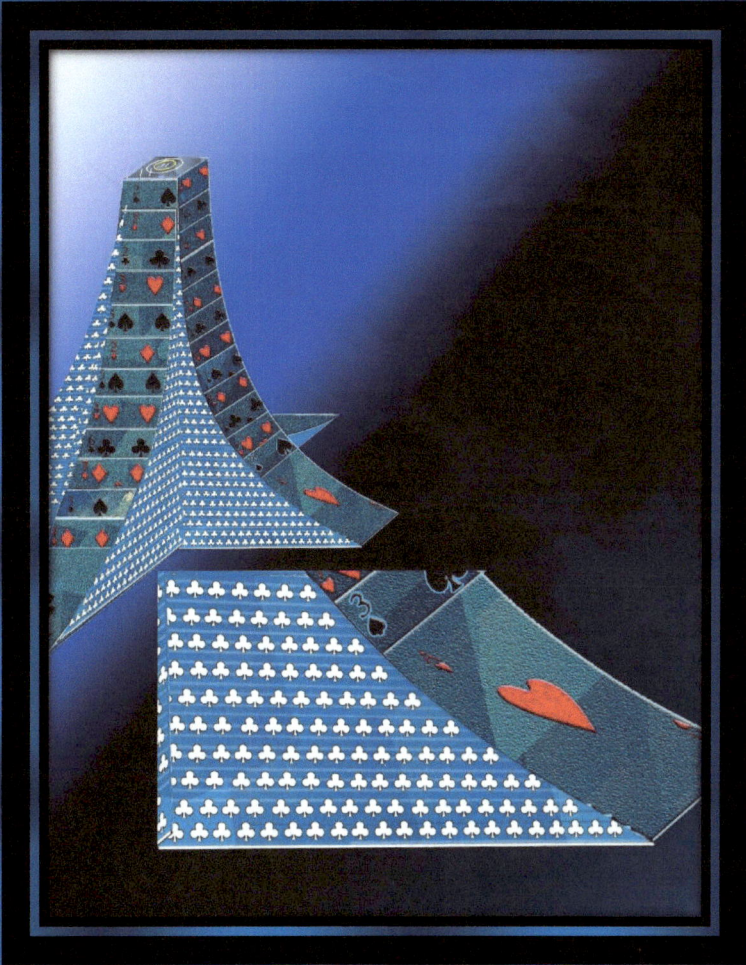

Windows can be made in two ways.

One is rectangular and the other is the shape of the name of that part of the building.

Building glasses are made of clear glass, which are solar panels. And this building doesn't need fossil fuels.

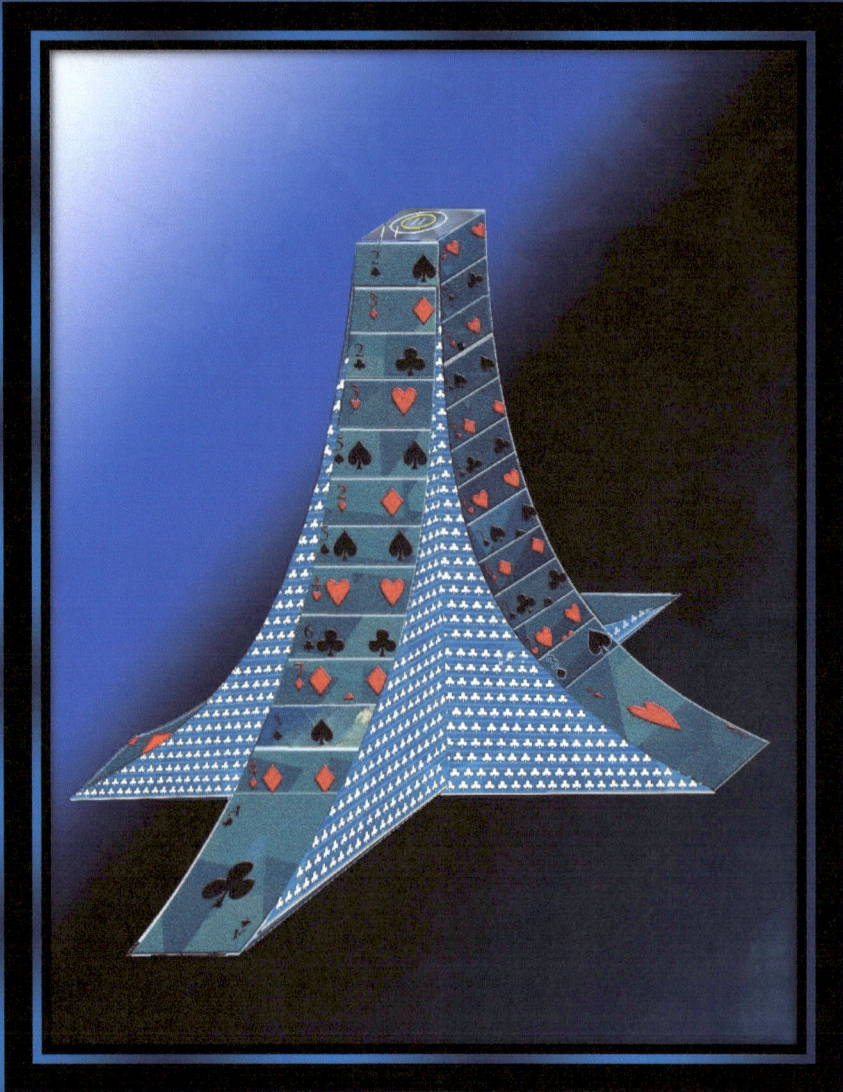

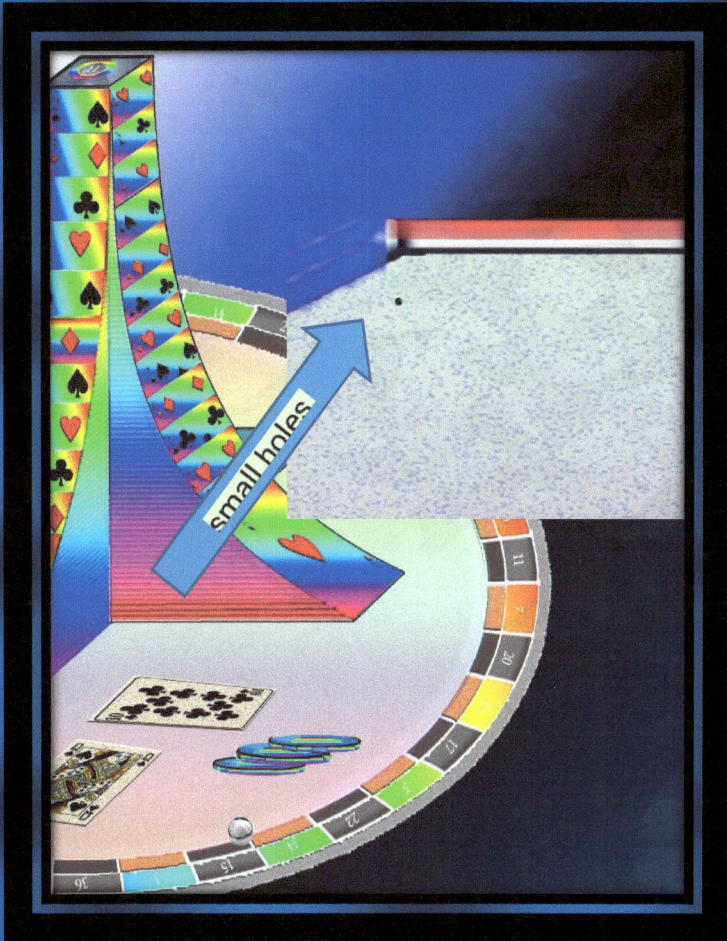

There are many small holes in the floor around the building, these holes direct rainwater in used after purification for drinking, bathing and washing.

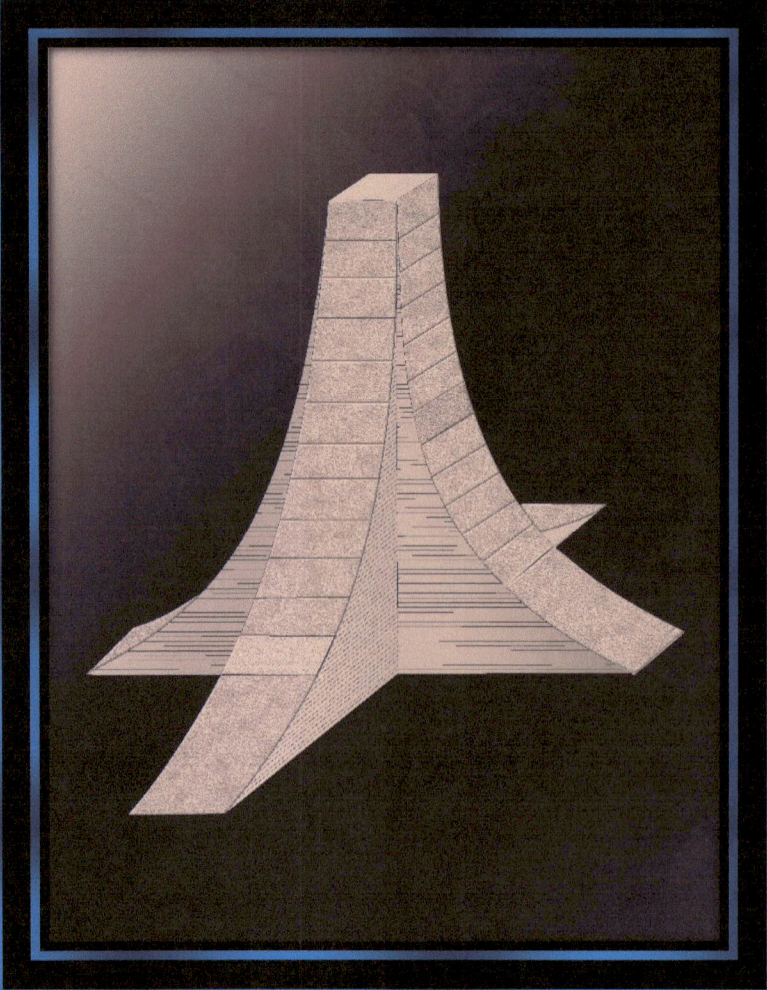

The walls of the building are heat and sound insulation and it will create a calm and pleasant environment.

There are several futsal halls, tennis courts, volleyball courts, basketball courts, etc. in the building.

There are two and three story building around the tower; which are designed in the form of casino chips.

These buildings are coffee shops and resturants.

These two and three story buildings can rotate.

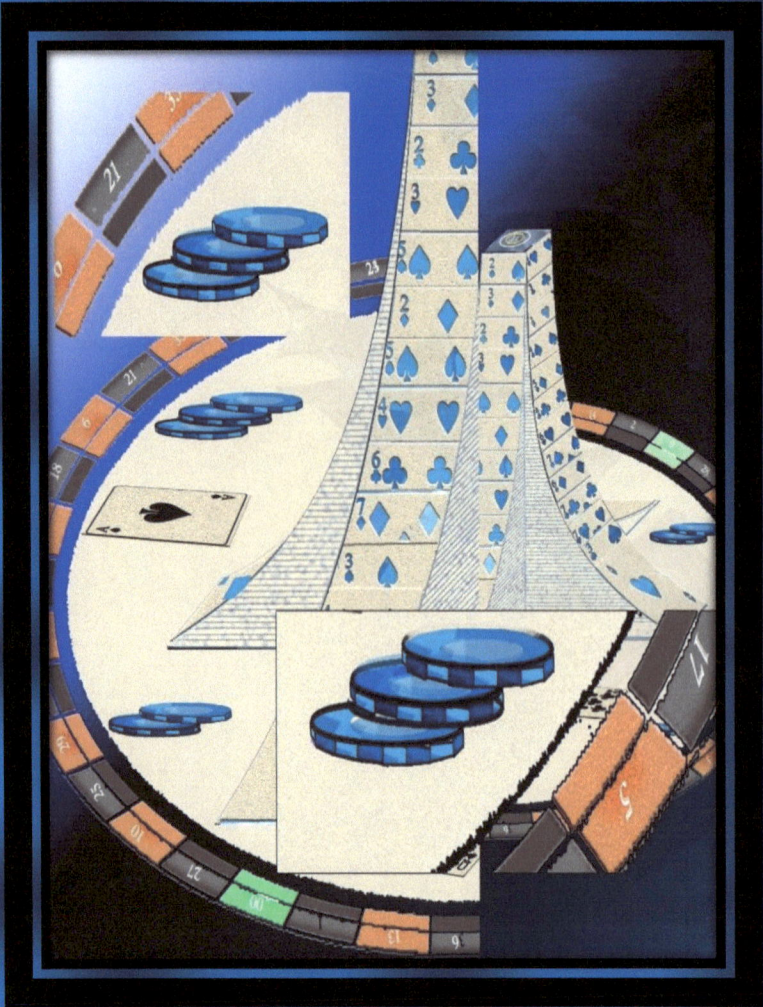

The building has a helipad too

16

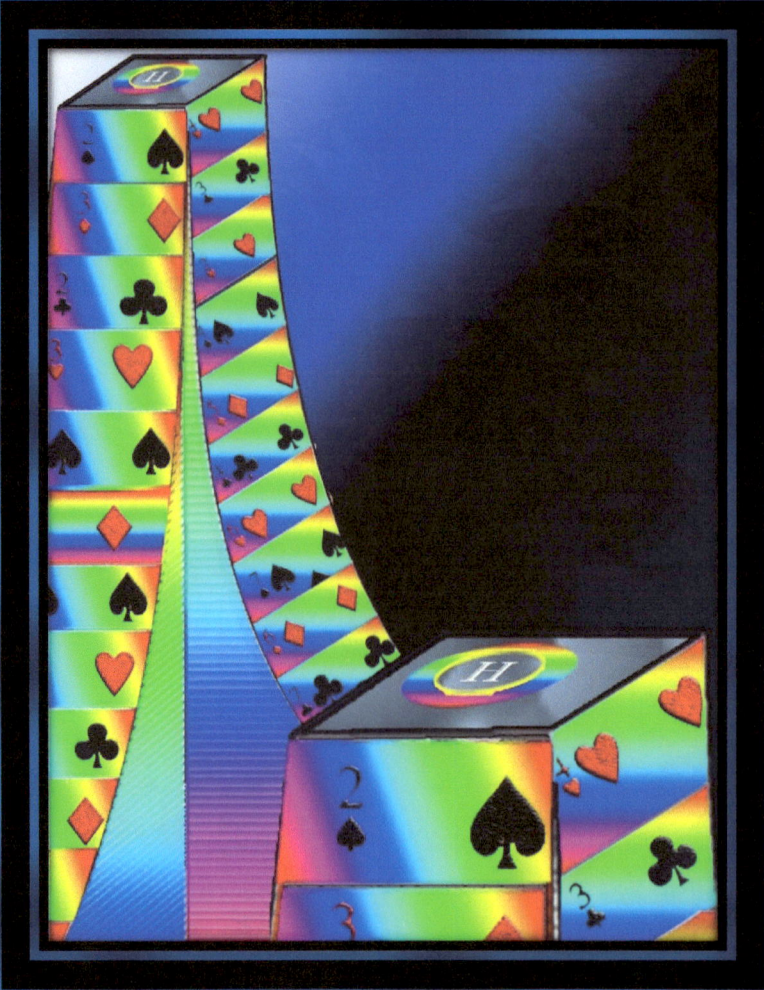

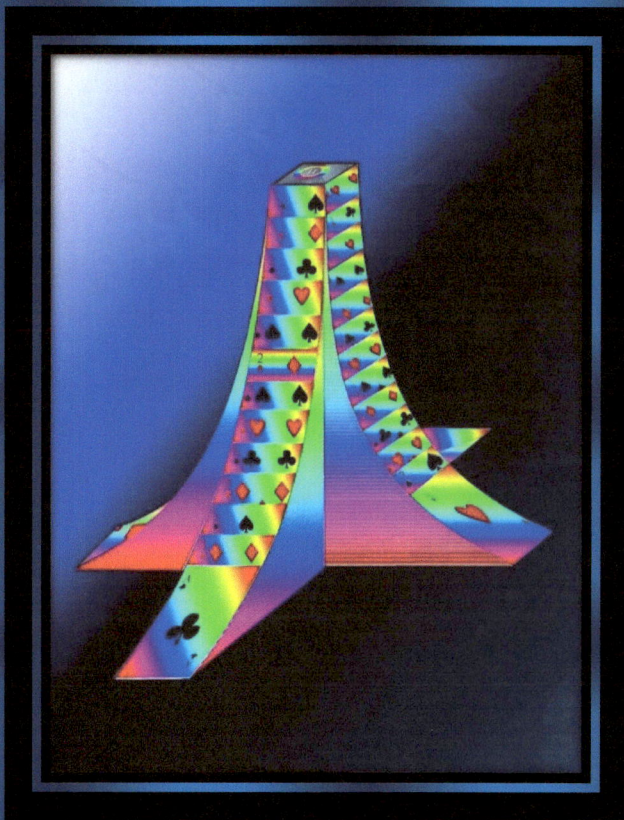

From the top view, a square roof can be seen and each side of the square continues with very beautiful curvature toward the ground.

Playing cards are arranged on this curvature and it's like that the cards slide over each other and come down.

The arrangement of the cards is random and it changes every hour. In fact, with each change of layout, it shows the passage of an hour.

This change is accompanied by the sound of the cards shuffle.

The darkness of the night causes the lighting look beautiful on the playing cards.

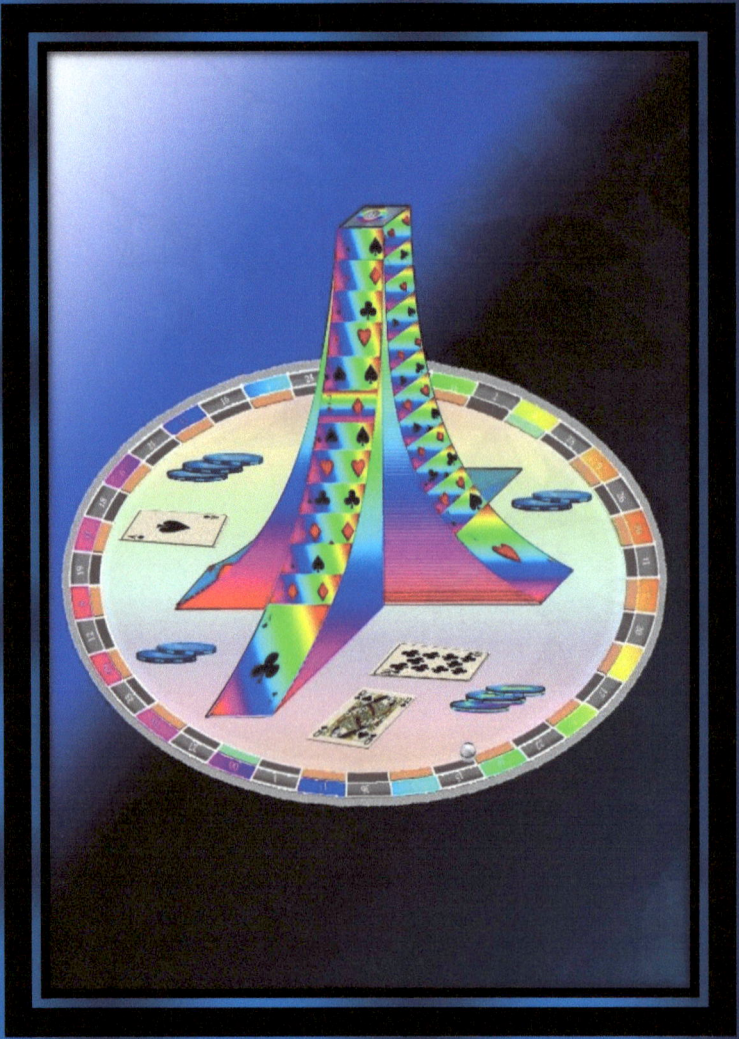

The area around the tower is designed in the shape of rotaiting roulette table.

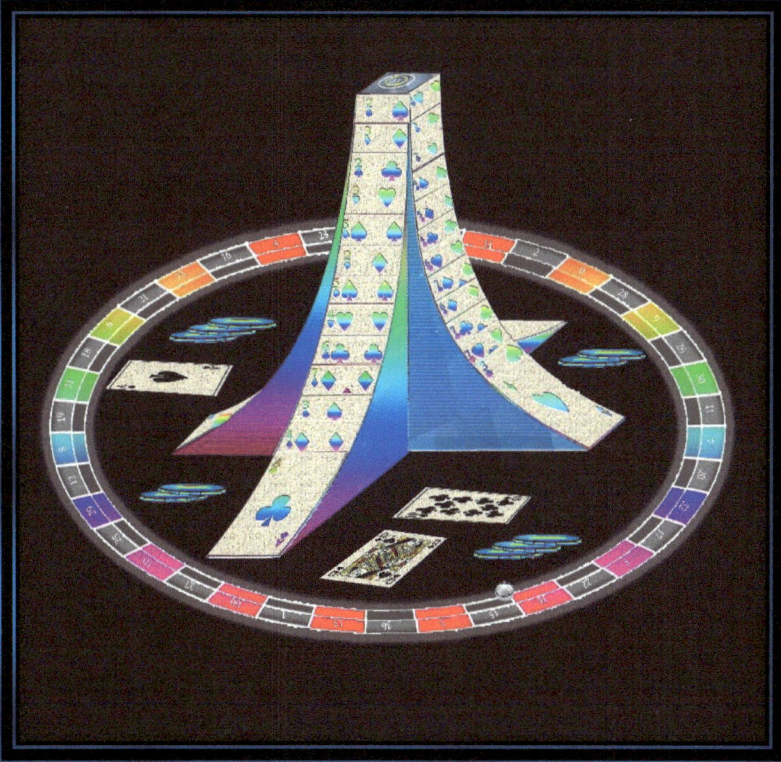

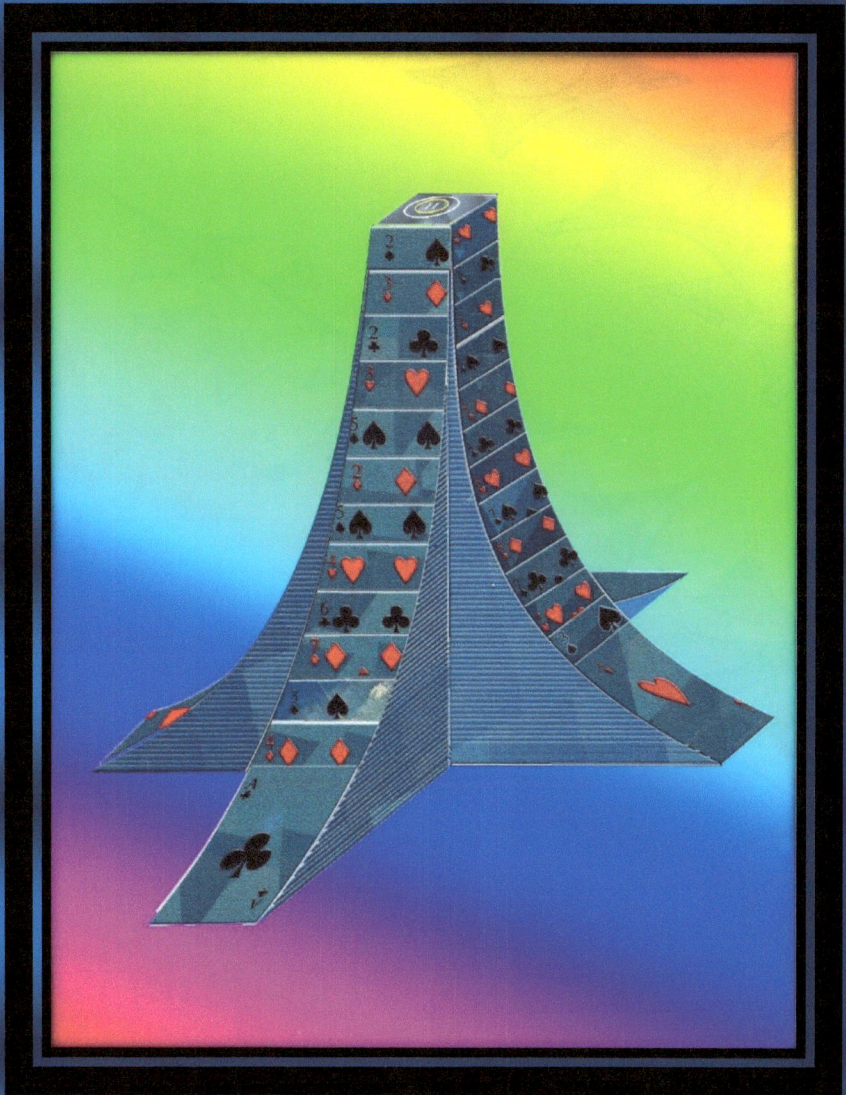

Glorious

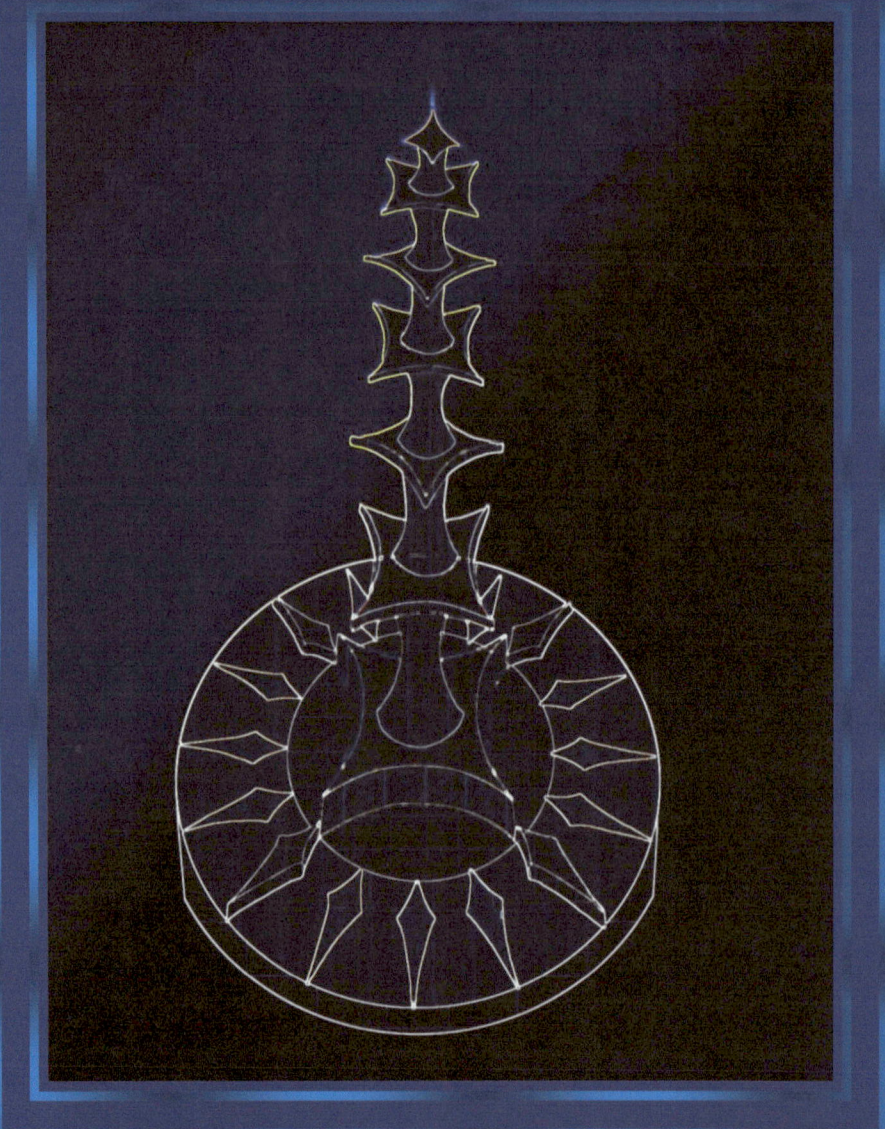

We were inspired by rotation of the earth and we designed the rotating building

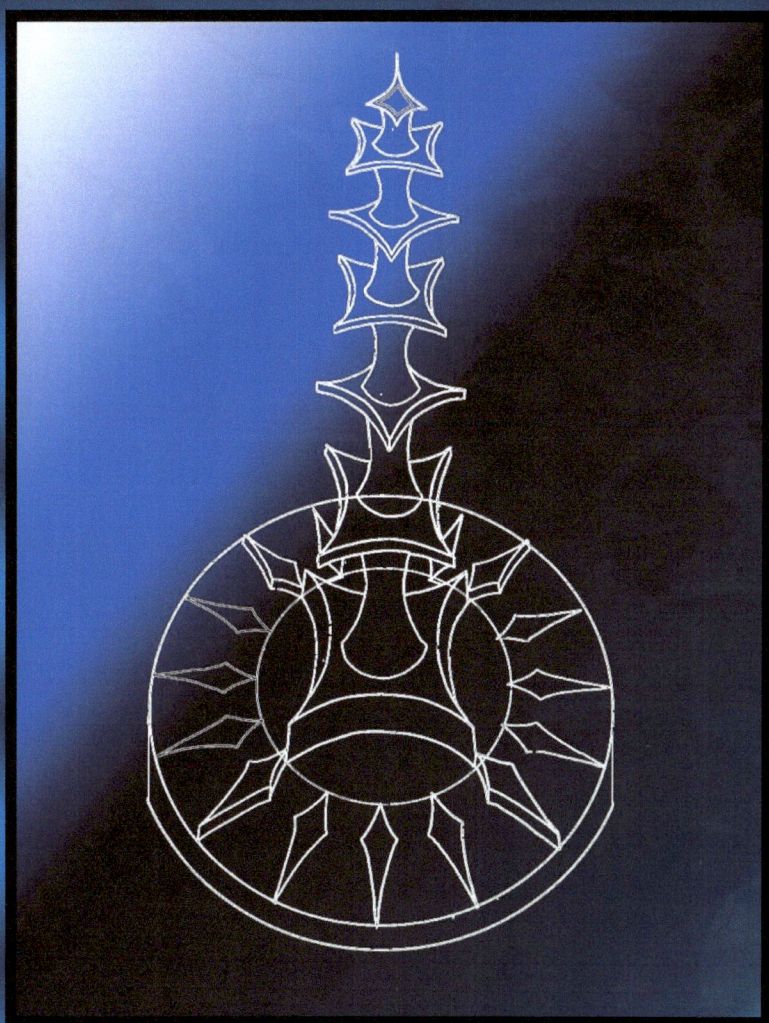

As the tower rotates, a different view will be visible from all around, during the day.

Building glasses are solar panels. These panels provide some of the tower's electrical energy.

The building is directed into underground reservoirs and then rainwater is purified.

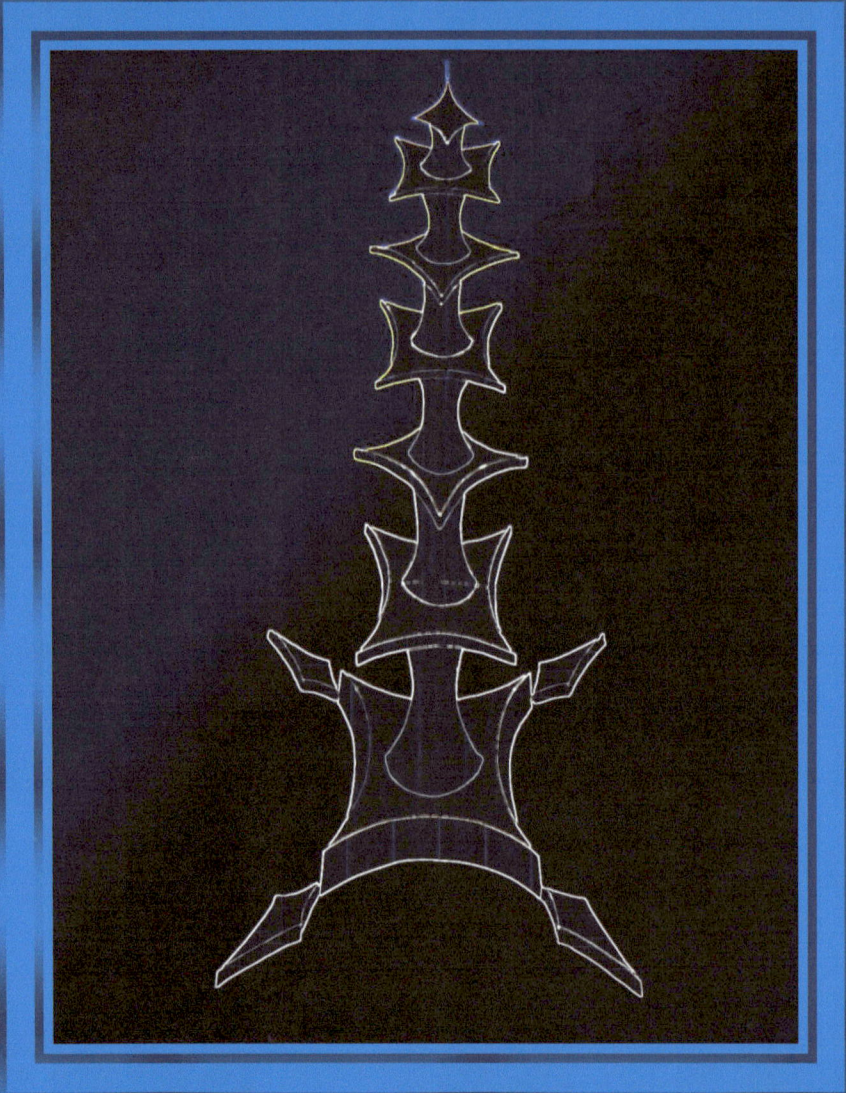

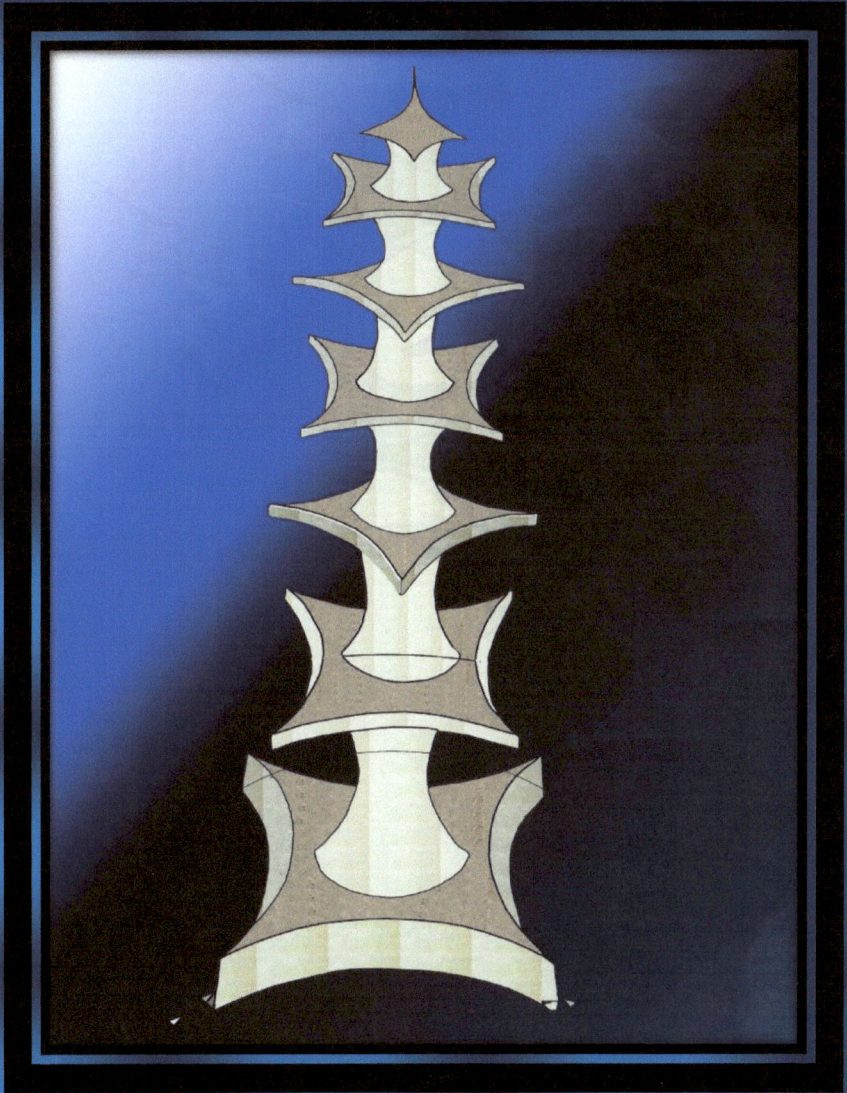

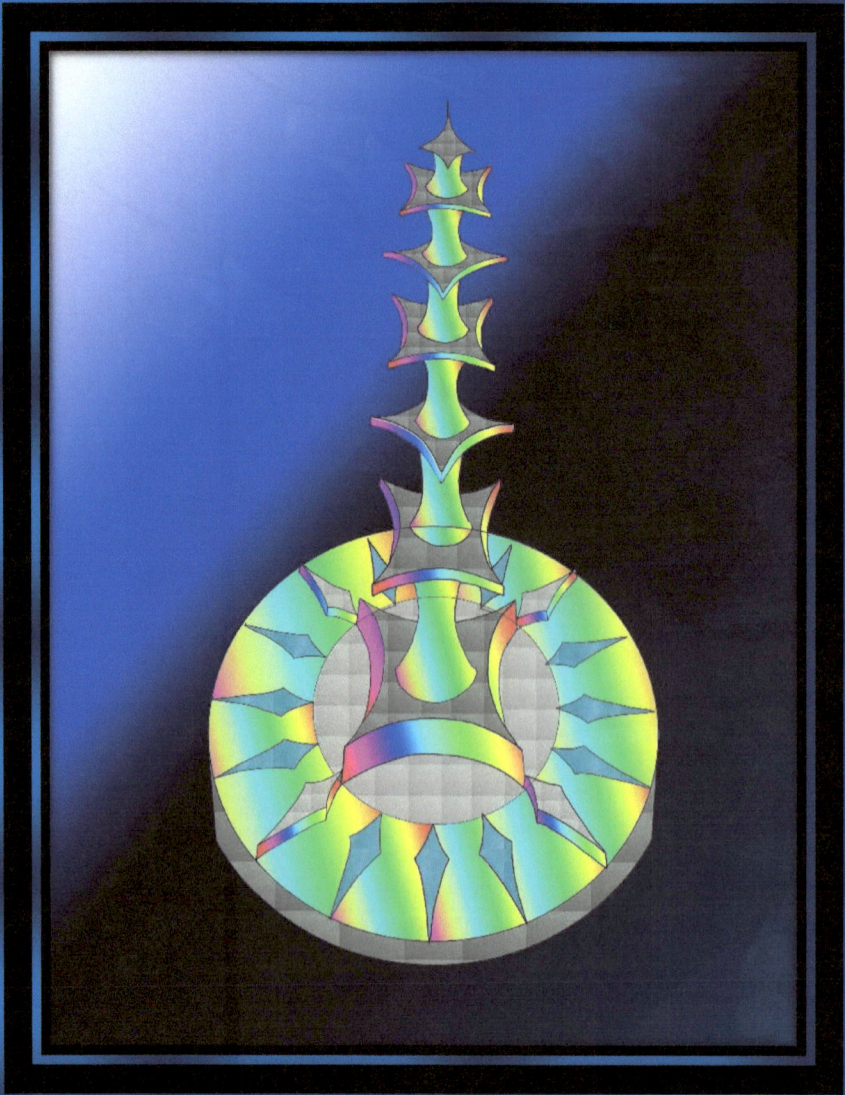

www.ingramcontent.com/pod-product-compliance
Lightning Source LLC
Chambersburg PA
CBHW041808040426
42449CB00001B/5